# 121 Reasons Why Every Woman Should Have A Gay Man In Her Life

Robert Steele

This book is dedicated to all the women in my life that have loved me for who I am; they are the inspiration for this book.

Monica

Eva

Kerrie

Dawn

Leanne

Marcy Judy

Michele

To Craig, the love of my life, who believed in this crazy idea for a book and supported me.

ISBN 978-0-578-00624-6

Copyright ©2008 by Robert Steele

All rights reserved. No portion of this publication may be reproduced, stored in a retrieval system, or transmitted in any form by any means—electronic, mechanical, photocopying, recording, or any other without permission from the publisher.

He goes to Celine, Madonna, Cher, and Bette concerts with you – and sings along with every song.

# 2

He goes shopping with you anytime, anyplace, and for no reason.

3

He tells you that your dress is fabulous – he should know because he probably has the same one.

4

He gets a manicure and pedicure with you (oh and don't forget the facial).

5

He tells you that the jeans make your butt look fat, and you won't get mad at him.

## 6

He goes with you to see any Broadway musicals.

# 7

# He agrees that McSteamy is hotter than McDreamy!!

8

He stands in the mirror with you and lip-sync Britney songs using your hairbrush.

9

He picks out the perfect shade of eye shadow to match your fierce outfit.

# 10

# He trains you to walk in 5-inch heels.

## 11

He watches 'Grease' with you, as long as he gets to sing all Sandy's songs.

12

He dishes the outfits from the red carpet better than those "so-called" fashion experts from entertainment shows.

# 13

# He agrees with you that men ARE pigs!!

14

He NEVER goes to Hooters, no matter how good the chicken wings taste (once again men ARE pigs!)

15

He is **always** ready to go dancing with you and the girls!!

## 16

He looks better in a tux than your boyfriend or husband.

## 17

He always compliments you – without being asked.

18

His hair is always in style (not parted down the middle and feathered – that is so 80's).

19

He knows how important it is to wear the perfect outfit just to go shopping.

# 20

He lends you his perfect little black dress.

## 21

He knows first hand that under-wire bra's are not comfortable.

## 22

He always shares his beauty tips with you.

23

He isn't ashamed to have cucumbers on his eyes while getting a facial with you.

24

He will go with you to Oprah's favorite things show.

25

He *ALWAYS* notices when you lost 5 pounds by saying: "Girl you are looking fierce. You lost some poundage!"

# 26

# He DVR's Ellen and Oprah.

## 27

He picks out the perfect nail polish to match any outfit.

28

He notices when you have a new haircut.

## 29

He can cut your hair (it is in his genes you know).

30

He has incredible rhythm on the dance floor (it is in his jeans).

## 31

He notices when you bought a new outfit, but will NEVER tell your husband or boyfriend.

## 32

He doesn't do the "White-man overbite" while dancing – he couldn't even if he wanted to.

## 33

He would rather watch Desperate Housewives than football on Sunday night.

## 34

He tells you that you look cute in your footy pajamas.

## 35

He lays around on a rainy day and watches 'Pretty Woman' with you, for the hundredth time.

## 36

He cries while watching 'Ghost'.

# 37

He critiques the evening gowns, shoes, and hair-do's and don'ts during beauty pageants.

## 38

He understands why you
need new shoes every season.

# 39

He actually opens the doors
for you.

40

He buys you beautiful flowers
without expecting sex
(chances are he has
rearranged the bouquet
before he gives them to you).

# 41

He tells you that you look fabulous at least once a week.

# 42

# He NEVER forgets your birthday!!

# 43

He bakes you a cake for your birthday, from scratch.

# 44

# He agrees that Diamonds are a woman's best friend!!

## 45

He always remembers your anniversary – and doesn't want sex.

46

He agrees that men should be more sensitive.

## 47

He agrees that "Sleepless in Seattle" is one of the most romantic movies.

## 48

He buys you male nudie magazines, without any complaints... DUH!

## 49

He buys tampons for you without complaining or being embarrassed.

50

He understands that all flavored condoms are not worth trying.

## 51

He tells you which edible body lotion won't leave a rash.

## 52

He understands the pain of shaving your legs (and underarms).

53

He takes you to art galleries openings, because a lot of other gay men are bringing their "girl friends" there too.

## 54

He goes to the newest trendy restaurant without complaining (because we all know that is where other hot gay men go).

## 55

# He agrees that John Bon Jovi is still HOT!!!

## 56

He knows that you make the buying decisions. He is just there to make sure you look good in whatever you decide to buy.

# 57

He smells hundreds of perfume samples to find the perfect scent for you.

## 58

He knows if you are a spring, summer, winter, or fall (try asking your husband or boyfriend that – see if they even know what it means).

## 59

He doesn't buy you sleazy outfits for your anniversary or birthday (well ok maybe he does, but he always wants to borrow them).

## 60

He does NOT buy you an appliance for ANY occasion (unless it is the newest-must-have hair appliance).

## 61

# He knows how to decorate a house.

## 62

He understands why the sheets need to match the comforter.

63

He agrees that the towels in the guest bath need to match – and yes they are for decoration ONLY!!

64

He **does** read Girly magazines for the articles.

# 65

He is sympathetic to the pain of walking in high heels, because he has literally walked a mile in your shoes.

## 66

He goes to every
Chick-Flick with you, usually
opening night.

## 67

He knows why you *can not* go out of the house without putting on your lips.

68

He cuddles in bed, without thinking it will lead to sex.

69

He shaves on the weekends –
everywhere.

## 70

He doesn't wear the same suit from 10 years ago, heck he threw that suit out 9 1/2 years ago – it was out of style after the first six months.

## 71

He takes you ballroom dancing (good luck deciding who gets to lead).

## 72

He agrees that you need a new bathing suit every year.

# 73

# He knows which bathing suit fits your body type

## 74

He uses the internet for shopping – and not for porn (well even if he did you wouldn't complain).

## 75

He goes to step aerobics with you, mostly to show off his new aerobic outfit.

76

He eats ice cream with you when you are soothing your stress, broken heart, weight gain – heck for any reason.

## 77

# He is sympathetic while you have PMS.

## 78

He knows the difference between panty liners and tampons.

## 79

He doesn't try to see if your deodorant *IS* strong enough for a man.

## 80

He picks out paint that matches the décor.

## 81

He talks all night about important life stuff like; what the upcoming fashions are; which soap opera hunk looks best without a shirt on.

## 82

He arranges the perfect floral arrangement for a dinner party.

## 83

He believes in maid services – because it gives you more time for shopping.

## 84

He pulls out your chair for you to sit down.

## 85

He shares his food without complaining.

## 86

He orders Cosmopolitans, because he loves holding the glass too, it is so gay!

*87*

He orders the latest fun martini.

## 88

He agrees there is such a thing as a too-short-of-a-skirt, especially for women over 45.

## 89

He goes to Karaoke bars with you – trust me you will have to drag him out of there (all pun intended).

## 90

He sings duets with you at Karaoke night. (Endless Love, Island in The Stream, It's Raining Men)

91

He doesn't wear the same ratty t-shirt from his college days – he burned it shortly after graduation.

## 92

He doesn't care about March Madness — only March sales.

## 93

He helps you find something to wear, especially when you "don't have anything to wear" (he will most likely let you borrow something of his to wear).

94

He understands why an inspiration piece is important to decorating a room.

## 95

He will color your hair because he believes grey hair only looks good on other people.

## 96

He writes lyrics to a 'he done me wrong' song with you.

## 97

He would choose Ben over Matt, but wouldn't kick Matt out of bed for eating crackers.

*98*

He orders salad dressing on the side, just like you.

## 99

He helps you pick out that perfect picture frame for that special picture.

100

He knows why you need a wrap dress in every color (boy those things travel well).

# 101

He knows how to pack
enough outfits for a week in
an overnight bag.

102

He knows how to tie a scarf into several different styles.

## 103

He can match his own clothes.

104

He knows which tie matches which shirt.

## 105

He is able to match colors – he knows complimentary colors.

106

He knows that stripes do not go with plaid (no matter what is in the magazines).

## 107

He only wears plaid if it is in style (now paisley is another story, it's NEVER in style).

## 108

He buys you that perfect little black purse, or he will lend you his.

## 109

He answers your four calls a day and always has something new to dish about in each call.

110

He watches college cheerleading competitions instead of college football.

111

He watches the Winter Olympics for the ice skating.

## 112

He watches home improvement television for the newest decorating tips – and of course the hot male carpenters on the shows.

## 113

He is able to go to a home improvement store without going directly to look at tools aisle. (But he does because that is where the HOT men are!)

## 114

He coordinates weekend shopping trips around the sales happening.

# 115

He loves playing the game, "Marry, Sleep With, or Send to an Island?"

116

He watches all the campy TV re-runs from the 70's. He acts out the Bionic Woman's running; and Wonder Woman's spinning – let's not forget the Charlie Angles pose with you.

# 117

He 'manscapes' more than he landscapes.

118

He watches the summer Olympics for the gymnastics competitions - and likes the men's shorts.

## 119

He doesn't get Hockey either
– the men have no teeth, how
unattractive is that.

120

He tells you he loves you without expecting sex.

## 121

He understands your moods (heck he has more PMS than most woman).

BONUS REASON

He will be the best friend you have ever had – like the sister you've always wanted.

www.ingramcontent.com/pod-product-compliance
Lightning Source LLC
Chambersburg PA
CBHW031602110426
42742CB00036B/681